Ranger's House is a red-brick villa, built around 1700 alongside the west wall of Greenwich Park, at the top of Croom's Hill, facing towards Blackheath. Between 1815 and 1896 it was the official residence of the Rangers of Greenwich Park, who were appointed by the monarch to care for the park. In the eighteenth century the house changed hands at least five times, the most celebrated owner being Philip Dormer Stanhope, fourth Earl of Chesterfield, who lived here from 1748 until 1773.

With this succession of owners and official residents, several fine collections of art and furniture came and went. As a consequence, unlike houses that have remained in the same family for generations, Ranger's House had no collection of its 'own'. From 1974 the Suffolk Collection of paintings was shown here, and in 2002 this house of collectors became the new home of the Wernher Collection.

Sir Julius Wernher (1850–1912) was one of a group of men who, when diamonds, and later gold, were discovered in South Africa, around the turn of the twentieth century, became wealthy and successful from mining them. Born in Germany, Wernher spent nine years in South Africa, then settled in London and developed a financial empire that made him one of the richest men in the world.

The works of art that he began to collect from around 1890 were installed at his London town house, Bath House in Piccadilly. In 1903, he also bought the country estate of Luton Hoo, in Bedfordshire. After the death of his widow in 1945, his son Harold moved the collection from London to Luton Hoo, which they opened to the public in 1950 as a memorial to his son Alex who died in the Second World War. Forty years later a family tragedy prompted the sale of Luton Hoo and many of the works of art, but fortunately the care of most of Sir Julius Wernher's own collection had been vested in a charitable trust, the Wernher Foundation, formed in 1981 by Sir Julius's great-grandchildren (the late Nicholas Phillips and the Butter family). In furtherance

Maiolica trefoil-shaped dish, or wine cooler, Durantino, c.1530

of the policy of enh houses for visitors, collection from the English Heritage long-term loan wit... Trustees of the Foundation to provide the third, and most lasting, home for the Wernher Collection at Ranger's House.

Quite apart from the intrinsic quality of the 700 works of art, many of which are of international significance, the Wernher Collection is of exceptional interest in the history of taste and collecting. Like the Iveagh Bequest at Kenwood in north London, formed around 1890 by the brewer and philanthropist Edward Cecil Guinness, first Earl of Iveagh (1847–1927), Sir Julius Wernher's collection is a rare survivor from this period. Both collectors belonged to a generation of men of industry, many newly ennobled, who sought to furnish their fashionable town houses with works of art.

Diamond and enamel pendant of the infant Christ, Spanish, 17th century

Unlike those of some of the other so-called 'Randlords' who became millionaires in the 1890s, Julius Wernher's collection went beyond the fashionable tastes for seventeenth- and eighteenth-century paintings. The distinguishing strength of his collection, and one that makes it more than a magnificent survivor, is its focus on early Renaissance Italian art, and the 'decorative' arts of jewellery, ivory carvings, bronze sculpture, enamels and ceramics. Wernher possessed a remarkable eye for the intricacies of materials and craftsmanship, and collected as he travelled.

On the first floor of Ranger's House, English Heritage has endeavoured to convey the particular qualities of Sir Julius Wernher's collection, and to complement it on the ground floor with the more fashionable paintings and furniture that once filled the reception rooms at Bath House, and later Luton Hoo.

THE LIFE OF JULIUS WERNHER

A Promising Start 

Julius Carl Wernher was born on 9 April 1850 in Darmstadt, capital of the independent Grand Duchy of Hesse in the German Rhineland. The Wernhers were a middle-class Lutheran family, long established in the region. Julius's father, Friedrich, was an engineer, and his grandfather and great-grandfather were both judges. His family seems to have been a stable and highly cultured one: Friedrich was interested in subjects that were later to fascinate Julius: music, fine art and geology. The family also had wide-ranging business connections. Friedrich himself was director of an ironworks, a cousin owned vineyards, and his wife's family ran a cloth manufacturing firm.

AKG, LONDON

When Friedrich became chief engineer of a railway company, the family moved to the Rhineland city-state of Frankfurt which then, as now, was the financial centre of Germany. The financial interests of this city were linked to a network that stretched across Europe, encompassing Paris, London and Vienna. Young Julius was developing into a talented and hard-working individual with a special aptitude for mathematics and languages, and the advantages of Frankfurt were not lost on him. He secured an apprenticeship at a bank in the city, and then, in 1869, at the age of nineteen, he moved alone to Paris after obtaining a post as bookkeeper at the Ephrussi Porgès bank.

Julius seems to have adapted easily and enthusiastically to life away from home. The regular and detailed letters that passed between him and his mother indicate a very close relationship between them and a secure and loving upbringing. Julius was much missed by his parents and sister – his mother wrote that his father felt the loss of Julius's 'light-hearted and happy approach'.

In 1870, he was required to return to Germany, but not to be with his family. The German states, led by Prussia, had invaded France, and as Frankfurt had been absorbed into Prussia a few years before, Julius and other young men were required to serve in the Prussian cavalry. In a matter of months, Prussia crushed France and then absorbed the other German states into a new Empire,

Above: Julius Wernher's father, Friedrich

Left: Romerberg, at the centre of Frankfurt am Main, where Julius grew up. Engraving, 1847

Opposite: Signed photograph of Sir Julius Wernher inscribed for Sir Percy Fitzpatrick, 1909

Below: Postcard showing a Wernher family house in Nierstein where Julius's cousin owned vineyards

Right: Paris during the Franco-Prussian War, 1870–71

AKG, LONDON

uniting Germany as a single country for the first time. Paris now became the centre of a murderous and destructive civil war. Julius arrived in France too late to see action, and instead endured several tedious months deep in the countryside as part of the occupation army. His letters home reveal his boredom and contain a stream of pleas for food, money, books and newspapers. They also reveal his sensitivity to the destruction that could be wrought by soldiers and politicians and to the suffering caused to civilians.

Once free of military service Julius left Germany once again – this time for London. No doubt the chance to gain experience in the world's greatest financial centre appealed to him. He moved into lodgings in Dalston in east London and set about learning English and using contacts from Paris and Frankfurt to gain a position. He soon obtained work as a correspondent with a German export firm in the City, but he had been there only a few weeks when he was offered a job that was to change his life. The Paris-based diamond dealer Jules Porgès, brother of the banker for whom Julius had worked, asked him to go out to South Africa to assist Porgès's partner, Charles Mège, in the buying of raw diamonds.

Jules Porgès, Julius's employer, then business partner and lifelong friend

Diamonds had been discovered two years before in the remote territory of Griqualand West, and a full-scale 'diamond rush' had developed. Julius's parents worried about the risks, but Julius himself saw, as he said in a letter to his mother, that 'in a relatively short time there is a chance of independence ... One wins nothing without daring, and there are few cases where chance offers itself as it does here ... There is always a risk or danger in every business, and that can never be a reason for keeping away from it. What reproaches I would have to make in later life if I let such an opportunity go by.' In November 1871 he set out by ship for Cape Town.

One of many letters from Julius Wernher in South Africa to his mother. He used the paper twice, writing crosswise across the original script

A Decade in The Diamond Fields

Gold rose diamond-set ring, enamelled in black and green (hinges open to reveal a portrait), 17th century

After thirty-eight days at sea, Julius and Charles Mège reached Cape Town, and from there made the rough five-week journey by horse and cart to the Diamond Fields. On their arrival, in February 1872, they found huge ramshackle encampments of tents and corrugated-iron or wooden shacks, built around the four great 'diggings' and housing nearly 2000 people. The diamond rush had attracted professional prospectors and amateur adventurers from all over the world, followed by an army of supporting traders – hotels, bars, brothels and purveyors of all the day-to-day provisions that even tent dwellers needed. The diggings were divided into tiny 'claims' of which no man could hold more than two (later ten). Each digging became a patchwork of many separate claims dug down by individual prospectors assisted by a few black labourers.

Julius's letters home contain colourful descriptions of his new environment. He was clearly shocked by the immorality of the white prospectors who, he wrote, 'drink and booze like animals'. The Boers, descended from Dutch farmers, he described as 'a race of terrific bodily strength, but extraordinarily limited spiritually'. Like any young man coming from the cities of Europe to undeveloped Africa, Julius was fascinated by the differences between the people and cultures. He wrote of the 'kaffirs' as they were known: 'They have a stature and symmetry of limb, and are so strong and muscular that it is a pleasure to look at these naked Apollos. Of course in the town they have to wear clothes.' He also wrote that 'they can work like no white man, but are dreadfully lazy and waste a lot of time'.

For their first year Julius and Mège lived in a tiny two-room canvas house of a type commonly sold to prospectors. There was constant discomfort from the endemic fleas, oppressive heat and dust storms in summer, and chronic haemorrhoids caused by the heat and sedentary lifestyle. Julius appears to have accepted these discomforts very stoically. From the beginning he displayed the qualities that were to characterise his life and to carry him steadily to business success: hard work and attention to detail; high intelligence and measured judgement; an understanding of the need to get along with all sorts of people and to be well thought of by them; and above all a driven fascination for the workings of money and the accumulation and investing of it. As he later wrote: 'I love work for its own sake ... and I am

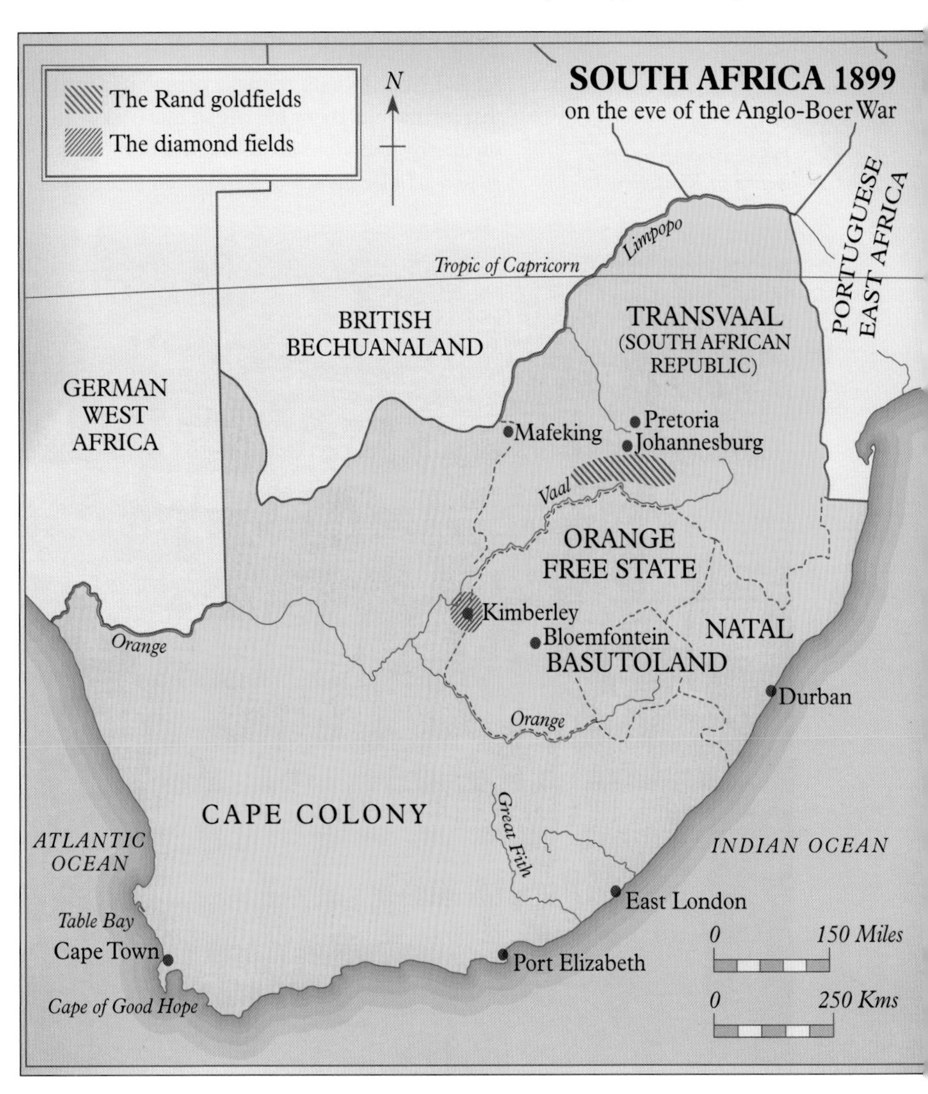

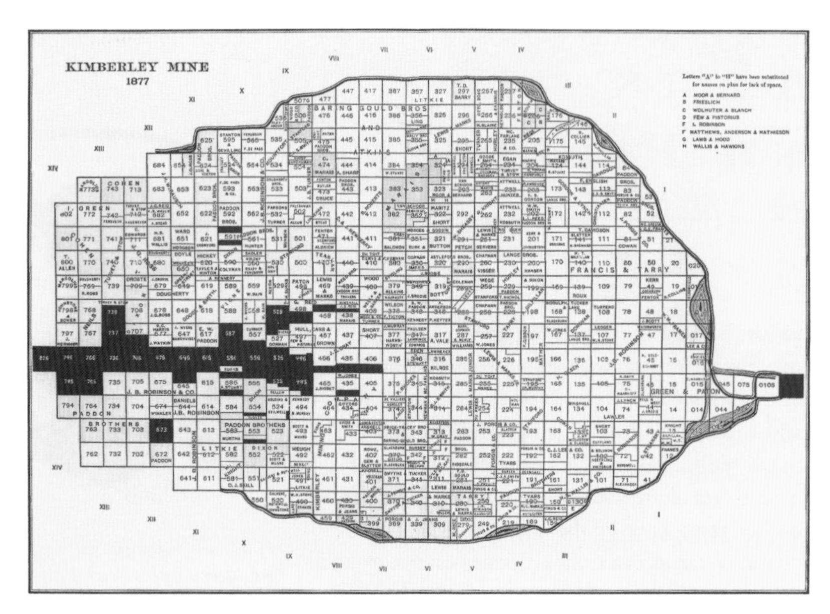

Above: Map of the 'claims' in the Kimberley mine, 1877, from The Diamond Mines of South Africa, *Gardner F Williams, New York, 1902*

Below: Mining and dry sorting in Kimberley, 1871

always pleased to be confronted by a quantity of it to get through ....' On another occasion, in answer to an aunt's criticism of avarice, Julius replied, 'it is difficult to make people understand that for the merchant his rise in material prosperity, therefore acquisition, is his aim, just as to a scholar his science and to an artist his ideal. It is only human not to stop and even a measure of success does not give full satisfaction.'

As for diamond buying itself, success depended entirely on selecting raw stones that could be cut and sold profitably back in Europe. The technical subtlety of this, as well as the instability of the prices, made it a very risky business. Wernher wrote: 'Everything depends on the right feel for it because the manifold varieties ... are so infinitessimal that it is quite impossible to learn by example. It depends on the form, colour, structure of the stone, purity, etc ... The shades are countless. Just as important is purity because from this one can determine what the stone will be like after it has been cut. The difference of opinion, even among the most eminent connoisseurs, is often enormous.' Despite this, within three months of arriving, he had learned enough from Mège to be trusted to start buying himself, as well as doing all the bookkeeping and domestic duties. Having mastered this essential skill, Julius was able, as planned, to take over as Porgès's sole buyer on the Diamond Fields when Mège returned to Europe late in 1873. Indeed, such

HULTON GETTY

THE BETTMANN ARCHIVE/BBC HULTON

Left: *Sorting diamonds in Kimberley, 1888*

was the trust that he engendered that, still only twenty-three, he was made a junior partner with a 25 per cent share of the profits from his buying. The Fields were growing into a permanent conurbation (offically renamed Kimberley), and Wernher now bought his own house, a small corrugated-iron bungalow, in its 'smart' district. He was also doing business on his own account (using capital borrowed on security of his family or saved as a result of his modest living), buying diamonds and the occasional claim, and importing beer and wine (the latter from his cousin's vineyards).

At first, Julius spent most evenings reading on his own, happy to avoid the gambling dens and brothels where many of the prospectors found their recreation. However, he soon became well known amongst the 'outlanders' and was often invited out to dinners and functions. Though many found him reserved, Julius enjoyed society and loved to dance and ride. Another diamond dealer observed, 'He never rode to the mines, or about the camp, except at a good hard gallop, and in the ballroom he flew across like a heavy dragoon in a charge.' When Julius later moved to a small house in Old De Beers, which he shared with three other young men and a

BARLOW RAND LTD

Below: *Julius Wernher's first home in Kimberley, 1873*

Spanish diamond and enamelled heart-shaped pendant, 17th century

Black workers at the washing equipment, Kimberley, 1870s

Right: 'The Big Hole' at Kimberley

KIMBERLEY PUBLIC LIBRARY

German cook, he admitted that it soon became something of a 'dovecote' for the curious young ladies of Kimberley.

No one thought the Fields would continue to yield stones for much longer and Wernher fully expected to return to Europe after a year or so. However, no matter how deep the diggings went, diamonds continued to be found. The network of diggings at Kimberley gradually developed into the biggest man-made chasm on earth and was known as 'The Big Hole'. It created a bizarre landscape, criss-crossed by wires and pulleys with thousands of men at the top pulling up buckets, or digging deep in the bottom of the pits. As the hole grew deeper, it became increasingly perilous for the diggers. Julius wrote that, 'Daily, men, carts and horses hurtled into the depths, and were dashed to pieces.'

Julius stayed on, doing steady business for Porgès and for himself through boom and slump until, despite competition from representatives of

Woodcut of 1872, from The Illustrated London News, *showing 'The Diamond Diggings, South Africa'*

AKG, LONDON

diamonds more cheaply. Porgès did just that, buying £90,000-worth of claims and allowing Julius to introduce new steam haulage and washing machinery. With this, Porgès became not just a diamond merchant but a mine owner, and naturally he put Julius Wernher in charge of this business.

Julius was now first and foremost a manager, although he still carried on diamond buying until another brilliant young German, Alfred Beit, arrived to take over this part of the business.

Above: English ladies of Kimberley sheltering from the sun

Left: Workers in a mine in Kimberley in 1873, with pulleys hauling rubble from the pit

many other European firms, theirs was the largest exporter of stones from the Fields. A turning point for Kimberley, and indirectly for Wernher, came in 1875 with the 'Black Flag Revolt' of prospectors who defied the British governor in an outburst against the commercial pressures on them. Their grievances included the governor's refusal to impose separate controls for black workers, and the interest rates demanded by the money-lenders. The prospectors were victorious in the short term – the governor caved in and banned blacks from owning claims by introducing passes and compounds to control black labourers. However, one other reform doomed the small prospectors. This was the lifting of the limit on the ownership of claims. The way was now open for men with capital to move in, buy up and consolidate claims into much larger mines, and invest in equipment to extract

Brought up in Hamburg, Beit was from a Lutheran background like Julius, and had studied diamond cutting in Amsterdam. He was to become Julius's closest friend and to remain so for life.

Julius's daily life was dominated by the direction of men and machines and the technicalities of mining – and by the imperatives of interest rates and share prices too. In order to raise the vast sums of money needed for this scale of mining, private partnerships like Porgès's had turned themselves into limited liability companies that raised capital on the European stock exchanges. Julius emerged as a masterful tactician who triumphed in the game of corporate draughts

AFRICANA MUSEUM

Above: Alfred Beit with pieces from his collection

Below: Dutoitspan Road, Kimberley, 1875

AFRICANA MUSEUM

that developed as companies competed to take over claims, with the aim of creating the biggest blocks.

By 1880 Julius determined to follow his long-cherished plan to leave South Africa and continue his career in London. The size and the international outlook of the world's biggest financial centre made it the obvious destination for a man of his experience and interests. Porgès readily accommodated his wishes by making him director of the London end of his 'French Company', and early in 1881 Wernher started work in the Company's Holborn Viaduct offices, near the Hatton Garden diamond district.

The Travelling Cabinet

In 1874 Porgès sent a very exotic Christmas present to Julius in Kimberley – a Louis XV mechanical travelling cabinet. It was a bizarre object to arrive in the rough mining area, but may have inspired Julius to begin collecting beautifully crafted works of art.

The cabinet was made around 1750–5, by Jean-François Oeben (1721–63). Another, almost identical cabinet is now in the Louvre in Paris.

Made of oak, veneered with tulipwood and purplewood, it opens out to act as a dressing cabinet or has a removable box that acts as a writing table. It reveals many fittings including three Chantilly porcelain containers painted with flowers, a small vase, a knife-handle, four spirit-flasks and a silver-mounted goblet, an engraved hexagonal glass and three items of cutlery with mother-of-pearl handles. The front has a sliding panel above a fall front and a drawer inlaid with cube parquetry. The removable writing box is leather lined with silver-plated fittings.

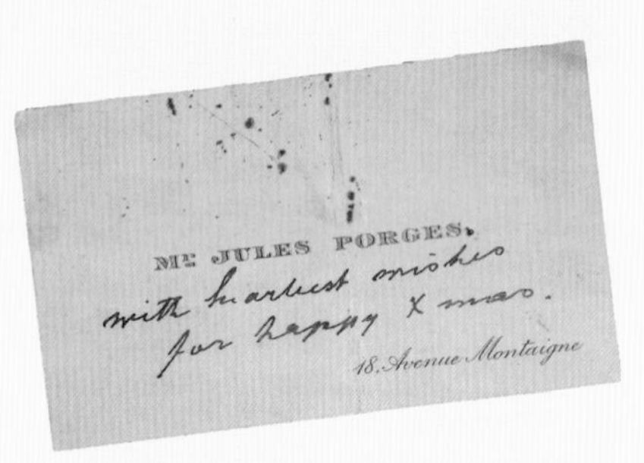
Mr JULES PORGES,
with heartiest wishes
for happy X mas.
18, Avenue Montaigne

Top left: Porgès's note to Julius, 1874

Above: Instructions for opening the cabinet

Left: The raised right shelf section showing a porcelain container and cutlery

Far left and left: The travelling cabinet closed and open

Below: The removable writing table

Gold, Mergers and Marriage

Left: Wernher, Beit & Co.'s offices in Johannesburg

Although Julius was based in London for the rest of his career, he continued to exert a key influence in the South African mining business. He communicated tirelessly by post and telegraph with his fellow directors in South Africa, particularly with Alfred Beit who was proving to be the most brilliant financial tactician of them all.

In Kimberley, diamond mining continued to concentrate in ever fewer hands – the French Company competed with several other major mining barons, notably Cecil Rhodes, Barney Barnato, and J B Robinson. The competition culminated in Wernher and Beit agreeing with Rhodes to amalgamate their respective companies and squeeze out the rest, until they had absorbed all the Kimberley mines in a single company, the famous De Beers Consolidated. In London, Julius was instrumental in creating the London Diamond Syndicate, a cartel which controlled London diamond prices and to whom De Beers sold exclusively. In effect, De Beers and Wernher's Syndicate between them had total control of the best part of the world's diamond production and sales, and could dictate prices accordingly. In 1889 Porgès retired to enjoy the fruits of his wealth, and sold his interests to a partnership of Wernher, Beit and two other mining managers in the fields, Max Michaelis and Charles Rube.

In 1885 there occurred an event that was to transform Wernher's life yet again and turn him into one of the richest men in the world: gold was discovered in South Africa on the 'Witwatersrand' ridge. It did not take long to realise that there were near-endless deposits of ore, but its poor grade and depth below ground meant that an enormous

AKG, LONDON

Cecil Rhodes, 1900, two years before his death at the age of 48

Below: Number 1, London Wall, Wernher, Beit's London office, is shown second from the left, next to the central office of Harry Oppenheimer

Right: Punch *cartoon of the infamous 'Randlord', Barney Barnato, 1896*

labour force and vast investment in equipment would be needed to extract it. If it could be mined cheaply enough, great wealth was assured for those involved, for the international price of gold was fixed and there was no danger of price slumps to undermine profits. There was no likelihood of opportunities for small prospectors this time – only those with access to great capital could even contemplate it. This is just what Wernher and the other diamond magnates had – and they were on the spot and experienced in the technicalities of mining as well.

The investors moved fast, and within a few years nearly all property on the 'Rand' had been acquired by the 'Randlords', as they came to be known: Rhodes, Barnato, Robinson, and most successful of them all Porgès, later Wernher, Beit & Co. From the beginning the income was great: as early as 1888 Porgès & Co. showed a profit of £860,000 (over £34 million in today's money). There were setbacks – work nearly halted in 1889 when they reached a type of ore from which gold could not be extracted until new chemical processes had been introduced – but generally it was a story of unprecedented success. Even the main investors did not have all the capital needed, and much more was raised by floating companies on the European stock exchanges. Gold share mania hit Europe and share prices repeatedly boomed and slumped. The handling of this aspect of the business became as important to the investors' success as the mining itself. In London, Julius Wernher was ideally placed to deal with this and became an expert – knowing which shares were worth buying when prices were low and which to sell when they were high. Not everyone was as scrupulous as Wernher, however, and South African shares became synonymous with dodgy dealing. The most infamous 'Randlord' was Barney Barnato who, on the verge of bankruptcy in 1887, mysteriously disappeared over the side of a ship on his way back from South Africa. But Wernher, Beit & Co. went from strength to strength. In 1893 the company floated its goldfield interests as the Rand Mines Ltd, and in two years its shares had increased in value 45 times. Alfred Beit was now reckoned the richest man in the world, with £10 million, while Julius Wernher commanded £7 million (equivalent to at least £280 million today).

Two postcards showing the development of Commissioner Street, Johannesburg, between 1887 and 1890

Marriage

Julius's total dedication to his business meant that he often worked in his office until midnight, seven days a week. This left him little time for courtship, but in 1886, a boyhood friend from Frankfurt, now living in London, introduced Julius to his sister-in-law, Alice Sedgwick Mankiewicz. Julius was thirty-six and she twenty-four. Alice, or Birdie as she was known, had studied the piano at the Royal

College of Music and could speak German, her father having come from a Prussian Jewish family. In December 1886 Julius began corresponding with her on the excuse of advising her on the resetting of some jewellery. His very formal letters would begin 'my dear Fräulein' and sign off, 'With kindest regards, Yours faithfully J. Wernher'. They corresponded throughout 1887 and Julius increasingly confided in Birdie his feelings about his business, his life and his friends. On her birthday in 1887 he gave her a topaz hatpin set in diamonds. Julius's devotion to business meant that he had to refuse several invitations to tea with Birdie, and then, in May 1887, with the death of his father in Frankfurt, he had to be away in Germany. Fortunately, Birdie's brother-in-law advised her to be tolerant, but Julius finally realised that the tone of her letters was becoming a little impatient. At this point he replied at once, this time ending, 'Good night, and god bless you, and keep me your love, Ever Yours Julius.' Three days later they became engaged.

They were married on 12 June 1888 at Christ Church, Lancaster Gate, and after the first week of their honeymoon, spent on the Isle of Wight, they were off to see Paris as guests of Jules Porgès. Here Birdie, who had lived with her widowed mother in part of a Victorian house in Bayswater, was 'dazzled' by the high society homes and art collections of her new husband's cosmopolitan friends, not least Madame Porgès, who is likely to have introduced her to her hallmark Worth dresses. She was soon to become a style-setter herself in London society.

Julius and Birdie moved into Porchester Terrace, Bayswater, where Birdie loved to entertain the international financiers of Julius's acquaintance. A year later, on 7 June 1889, their first son, Derrick, was born. He proved to be a disarmingly beautiful child whom everyone adored. In 1891, when Derrick was only two, Julius wrote to Birdie from abroad:

> 'The great fear is how he will turn out … I would not like a child of mine to be a useless self-indulgent idler simply because he is left so much a year – my pride would be to have a man as a son who will take his place in the world!'

Unfortunately Julius's fears were to be strangely well-founded, but he never admitted this until it was too late. Two more sons were to follow: Harold, born in 1893, and Alexander in 1897, but Derrick was always the favourite. Nicknaming him 'Sweetface' and constantly indulging him, Julius always cherished hopes of handing over the business to him. Even when Derrick began to disappoint him, Julius remained blind to the fact that Harold was the more stable character with the head for business. Like so many boys born at this time, Alex was to be killed in the First World War, at the age of nineteen.

Alice Mankiewicz
Julius Wernher
Verlobte
London S.W. 56 St. James Street
im März 1888.

Card announcing the engagement of Julius Wernher to Alice Mankiewicz, 1888

Left: Birdie and Julius on their honeymoon in 1888

Far left: Birdie with her sons Derrick and Harold in 1895

Below: Alex Wernher in uniform

High Society and Political Controversy

Below: Lady Caroline Price *by Sir Joshua Reynolds (1723–92) 1787. This painting hung in Bath House*

Right: Lady Wernher *by John Singer Sargent (1856–1925), 1902*

Below: Bath House, 82 Piccadilly, decorated for King Edward VII's coronation in 1902

Financial success opened the way to social success, and the acquisition of Bath House, a grand building in the millionaire district of Mayfair, helped to attract the high society that went with it. Julius even began to move in royal circles: in January 1897 he was summoned to see the Prince of Wales, at Marlborough House, together with Lord Rothschild and the banker E A Hambro, to discuss plans to mark Queen Victoria's Diamond Jubilee later that year. All must have gone well, for in June, Julius and Beit stayed with the Prince on his Norfolk estate, Sandringham, and were subsequently entertained again at Marlborough House. Birdie could not be invited until she was presented at Court, a formality that did not take place until 1898. She might anyway have been unable to attend, as their third child, Alex, was born in June 1897.

The Prince's scheme for a Hospital for Officers was also supported by Julius. His philanthropy was to be recognised with a baronetcy in 1905. According to *The Tatler*, reporting the honour, 'He is a great collector of pictures and has done a good deal in an unostentatious way for the advancement of higher education.'

An image of Julius and Birdie as hosts at Bath House is vividly painted in the diary of the social reformer Beatrice Webb. With her husband Sidney, she had successfully recruited Julius to back a campaign to create a college of science, Imperial College, founded in 1907 for London University. Julius had already been a guest of theirs, along with Lord Lytton and George Bernard Shaw, and returned their hospitality in May 1906. After their evening at Bath House, Beatrice described Julius in her diary as 'a German giant, not unduly self-indulgent, and a real drudger at his business' who, from his commitment to the commercial world of South Africa, was 'perpetually carrying the weaker men on his back'. She noted his remark: 'I have no time even to know that I am wealthy.'

She was far less charitable about Birdie, but then Birdie's love of ostentation and the opulence of Bath House were unlikely to have impressed these social reformers. Beatrice wrote:

'We went there… partly from curiosity to see inside such an establishment. … Though our host was superior to his wealth, our hostess and her guests were dominated by it. … The company was composed, either of financial magnates, or of the able hangers-on of magnates. The setting in the way of rooms and flowers and fruit and food and wine and music, and pictures and works of art, was hugely overdone …'

A Gentleman and a Lady at a Virginal *by Gabriel Metsu (1629–69)* c.1667, *purchased in Paris 1900*

The Pink Drawing Room at Bath House, 1911, photographed by Harry Bedford Lemere, (1865–1944)

NATIONAL MONUMENTS RECORD

The Entrance Hall of Bath House decorated for Queen Victoria's Diamond Jubilee, 1897

Birdie, 1892

Birdie did become well known for the lavishness of her entertaining. Her reception rooms were among the most elegant of the day with their glittering chandeliers, their backdrop of old master paintings and the sparkling display of porcelain which became an important collection in itself. According to a society journal of 1899, Birdie looked 'quite regal' at one Bath House reception, in a white brocade gown among 'a revelry of carnations arranged in graceful crystal and gold receptacles' complete with the relative novelty of electric light to 'set off every object in the room to brilliant advantage'.

The Honourable Henrietta Hanbury-Tracy *by Sir William Beechey (1753–1839), which hung in Bath House*

Political Controversy

Financial success also brought political controversy. The Anglo-Boer War between 1899 and 1902 caused great consternation in Britain with many blaming the 'Randlords'. Julius could not escape the criticism of some newspapers and politicians. The South African gold mines were at the heart of it. Unlike the diamond mines, which were in the British Cape Colony, the gold mines were in the independent Boer republic of Transvaal. The Boers were in two minds about the mines: they welcomed the taxes they generated but they feared that the great influx of 'outlanders' brought by the mines would eventually take over their land. As for Wernher and the other main investors, the commercial success of their mines depended on minimising

Left: Alfred Beit, Lionel Phillips, WA Walton, George Farrar, Abe Bailey and Frank Rhodes in Johannesburg, 1895

their enormous operating costs. To do this, favourable local administration and laws were essential, but the Transvaal government could not be relied upon in this respect. The government monopoly of the railways and of dynamite and cyanide supplies (key materials for gold mining) pushed up mining costs. Above all, the mines needed a constant supply of cheap black labour, but not enough black farmers were willing to leave their land for the mines; the Transvaal was reluctant to introduce new laws to deprive blacks of their land, and in effect force them into the mines.

Cecil Rhodes – whose ambitions were overtly political – took matters into his own hands. On 29 December 1895, a colleague of Cecil Rhodes, Dr Leander Starr Jameson, having grown impatient with the procrastinations of the reformers, launched an armed uprising in an attempt to overthrow the Transvaal regime. It was a failure – the agitators were easily suppressed by the Boers – but it caused political uproar in England and meant that even mine managers such as Julius Wernher, who had been determined to keep the peace if possible, would never be trusted again. Julius, in England throughout the episode, was fortunate not to be directly implicated or called upon to give evidence. His view was that 'The patient work of years is destroyed in a day.'

In the end the 'Randlords' got their way. An imperially minded British government appointed the aggressive Sir Alfred Milner as their South African High Commissioner. Milner, in collusion with the 'Randlords', placed pressure on the Boers and made war almost inevitable. In 1899 the British Army invaded the Transvaal, and the Rand goldfields were soon occupied. The Anglo-Boer War was to last another two years: the Boers took to guerrilla warfare and the British responded with a scorched earth campaign in which the Transvaal was ruined and thousands of Boers died of disease in British prison-camps.

The mining companies gained complete control of the goldfields and soon brought output to new peaks, but at a political cost, for the war shocked the world and divided Britain. Conservatives viewed it as an imperial triumph while Radicals and Socialists decried it as a capitalist plot, and the mining companies as the evil driving force behind it. The growing criticism of the political and financial power of the 'Randlords' deepened from this point.

Cecil Rhodes caricatured as the King of Diamonds

Caricature of Salisbury, Chamberlain and Rhodes during the Boer War: 'War and Capitalism or the transformation of blood into gold', Der Wahre Jacob, *1899*

AKG, LONDON

THE COLLECTOR

Bronze statue of Saint Sebastian, German, 1520–30

Right: The Spanish masterpiece St Michael triumphant over the Devil, *by Bartolomé Bermejo (1460–98), bought by Wernher (now in the National Gallery, London)*

Opposite: Julius's 'Red Room' photographed in 1911 by Harry Bedford Lemere

Below: Dr Wilhelm Bode in 1925. Bode advised Wernher on his collecting

Jules Porgès had always sought to encourage Julius Wernher's taste for beautiful craftsmanship and continued to encourage his former protégé by introducing him to other collectors and dealers in Paris. In 1891 Porgès even took Julius on a 'bachelors' holiday': a personal Grand Tour of Italy. Porgès was a great collector himself, with a taste for eighteenth-century French furniture and paintings, and seventeenth-century Dutch and Flemish pictures, in keeping with the fashion of the day. His was not a collection of particular distinction; indeed, Beit wrote in 1897 that Porgès had visited London and bought his 'usual rubbish'.

The most influential Parisian collectors visited by Julius were the brothers Rodolphe and Maurice Kann, financiers from Frankfurt to whom he had turned for investment in the new companies. Rodolphe Kann's collection was unusual in including early Renaissance works by Ghirlandaio and Bellini and Italian Renaissance bronzes. The Kanns suggested that, like Porgès, Julius should seek the advice of Dr Wilhelm Bode, then curator of paintings and sculpture at the Prussian Royal Picture Gallery in Berlin. Bode was in the habit of giving his advice to collectors in return for donations to his museum. Julius therefore wrote to Bode in June 1889, and offered two paintings. In return, Bode did advise Julius but found him to have a considerable degree of discernment of his own where works of art were concerned. Julius's training as a diamond buyer had taught him to scrutinise each work of art individually for skill in execution and condition, before considering its worth. Unlike collectors such as Beit and J Pierpont Morgan, whom Bode also advised, Wernher never bought in bulk on trust, and did not depend on any one expert adviser or dealer. Lord Carmichael, a Trustee of the National Gallery, wrote to Birdie in 1925 that his friend 'was always willing to listen to anyone in whose knowledge he believed, but I don't think he often took advice unless he was quite convinced himself'. Carmichael recalled that Julius was remarkably 'careful as to what he

AKG, LONDON

NATIONAL GALLERY, LONDON

did buy … he made a rule of buying nothing which did not seem to him to raise the standard of his collection as a whole'.

Acquired in London, Paris, Rome, Frankfurt and Berlin between 1890 and 1910, Julius's collection had a definite Continental flavour. This was at least partly because Julius was always very aware of his German background.

Julius Wernher's collection has two distinct strands, one reflecting his own eclectic taste in works of art, and the other the fact that he owned a home which must be stocked with furniture and paintings befitting the tastes of the day. He also occasionally bought items specifically to appeal to Birdie. The most distinguished parts of the collection are therefore the Medieval and Renaissance works which particularly interested him. The eighteenth-century items are more typical of the works gathered by dealers for the newly wealthy and ennobled merchants finding their way into London high society.

Above: The Rest on the Flight into Egypt *by Filippino Lippi (*c.*1457–1504), bought by Wernher in 1898*

Above right: Limoges enamel plaque of Thisbe by Léonard Limousin, c.*1530*

Right: Oval dish moulded with marine life by Bernard Palissy, 16th century

Below: A Sèvres vase, 1768, bought by Wernher in 1895

Typical of Julius's taste for unusual early works of art was the late fifteenth-century Spanish masterpiece of *St Michael triumphant over the Devil* by Bartolomé Bermejo, on which he sought Bode's advice when purchasing it in 1899. The same fascination led him to purchase the famous painting *Christ taking Leave of his Mother* by Albrecht Altdorfer in 1904. Both paintings are now in the National Gallery, London. By contrast, Julius purchased a view of Eton College by James Baker Pyne, possibly as a gift for Birdie on the birth of their second son, Harold, and then, in 1895, Watteau's *La Gamme d'Amour* (also now in the National Gallery). In 1898 Julius bought *The Rest on the Flight into Egypt* by Filippino Lippi, which Kann had recently sold to the dealers Agnew.

Today, the collection is best known for the diversity of Medieval and Renaissance pieces (see pages 28 to 35).

Following Kann's example, Julius bought bronze statues, particularly at the vast sale in Paris in 1892 of the dealer Frederich Spitzer. At the same sale, he bought a Limoges plate signed by Pierre Raymond, a sixteenth-century German clock and wax portrait, a baroque enamelled pearl pendant, and more.

The one surviving notebook recording Julius's collecting during the years 1893 to 1897 identifies 230 items, none of which were paintings. Jewellery was a favourite field, and the other main focus for his attention was ivories from the Byzantine, Carolingian and Romanesque periods. His love of intense details and the most skilful craftsmanship also led him to collect silver-gilt, blue Sèvres porcelain, Hispano-Moresque ceramics, Palissy ware, German stoneware, clocks and tapestries.

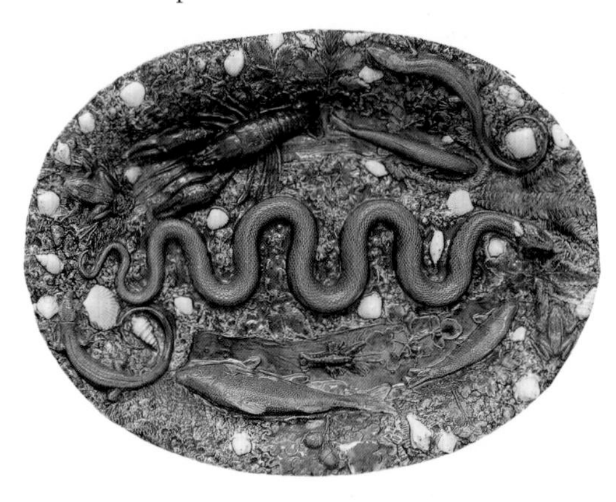

A legend grew up that he was so busy with his business that he could only see dealers over breakfast. This seems to have stemmed from a recollection by Lord Carmichael that he used to tease Julius for putting breakfast before art. He wrote:

'He said it was because porridge always made one feel that it was well not to be over extravagant.'

In April 1896, the purchase of the lease of Bath House, 82 Piccadilly (demolished 1960), on the corner of Bolton Street opposite Green Park, gave Julius the chance to have a private 'museum room'. Here he could display the more unusual works of art that would look out of place downstairs, but the new house also necessitated the acquisition of paintings and French furniture on a grand scale for the living rooms. It appears that the ground floor, with its elegant Pink Drawing Room (see page 15) and Yellow Drawing Room, aspired to emulate the Marquess of Hertford's house nearby in Manchester Square, which opened to the public as the Wallace Collection in 1900.

La Gamme d'Amour (The Scale of Love) *by Jean-Antoine Watteau (1684–1721), 1715–21. Bequeathed by Wernher to the National Gallery, London*

Julius's museum room, the 'Red Room', was situated upstairs, presumably to provide a refuge from the demands of business and society. In marked contrast to the silk, marble and chandeliers of the reception rooms, with their portraits of eighteenth-century society ladies such as the Countess of Bellamont and of Birdie, a set of photographs, taken in 1911, reveals that in the Red Room pride of place was given to Titian's portrait of the Genoese merchant Giacomo Doria (now in the Ashmolean Museum, Oxford).

The arrangement of the collection evidently gave Julius as much, if not greater, pleasure than the acquisition of individual works. As shown in the photographs and inventories, the effect is unusually dense, and the objects are not grouped by period and materials, as in most museums, but mixed together for effect. Julius once remarked, 'Every vitrine must be like a picture.' Lord Carmichael recalled that when he did buy something:

'They were always objects which harmonised with others which he used to refer to as "splendidly ugly". We used to congratulate each other because we both like the "splendidly ugly". He said, I think probably with truth, it was because we felt that such had been made by stronger and more thoughtful workers than many objects which appeal by the extreme delicacy and beauty of their finish; no one knew better than he did how to use it in juxtaposition when arranging his collection.'

Twenty-six paintings hung in the room, mostly in two tiers on brass chains, the larger works above fitted with individual picture lights more elaborate in design than the lights downstairs. Below, in finely carved, velvet-lined cabinets, some fitted with mirrors, stretched a twinkling array of ivories, bronzes, Limoges enamels and maiolica. Together with the red damask wall hangings and Eastern rugs, the room must have resembled the treasury of a Renaissance prince.

There were similarities between Wernher's collection and those of the great contemporary American collectors, notably J Pierpont Morgan, Henry Clay Frick and Henry E Huntington. Julius Wernher made no provision for a museum in his name – his collection was a highly personal one formed for the pleasure it gave him.

Left: Maiolica footed dish painted with a dog attacking a rabbit, Siena, c.1500–20

Below left: Gold oval locket enclosing a minute ivory Crucifixion, Spanish, 17th century

Below: A German silver-gilt mounted coconut cup formed as an owl – one of the most unusual and endearing pieces in the collection, 19th-century replica of a 17th-century design

LUTON HOO

Below: Shooting party at Kyllachy, Berwick, in 1901 including Julius with Harold over his knee, Derrick blowing the trumpet, Maria Wernher (left) and Franz Mankiewicz (right)

Julius did try to allow himself some recreation as a break from his business. As well as mingling with his and Birdie's friends at Cannes and Biarritz and 'popping over' to Paris regularly, Julius sometimes escaped to Scotland in the summer for country sports with his sons, or rented country houses for weekends.

From the late 1890s, the Wernhers rented a rural retreat of their own. Luton Hoo was a country house and estate of 5218 acres between Luton and Harpenden. This would provide a perfect 'weekend retreat' for golf and pheasant shooting. Julius and Birdie may also have been mindful of the necessity of returning the hospitality of the Prince of Wales.

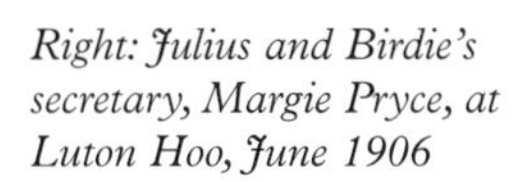

Right: Julius and Birdie's secretary, Margie Pryce, at Luton Hoo, June 1906

The owner of the house was the wealthy widow of the Danish Ambassador de Falbe. When Mrs de Falbe died in 1899, Julius purchased the marble sculpture by F Bergonzoli, *The Loves of Angels*, at the auction of Luton Hoo's contents: it is still part of the collection. He then decided to buy the house and completely remodel the interior in the fashionable Louis XVI style.

Below: Luton Hoo in Bedfordshire, bought by Julius Wernher in 1903

Luton Hoo had been remodelled by the architect Robert Adam from 1766–74 and later modified in part by Robert Smirke, before being gutted by fire in 1843. It was then rebuilt, and its owner, John Leigh, even provided his own railway station for the use of royal guests at the society balls hosted here.

The Wernhers engaged the fashionable Paris architect Charles Frédéric Mewès, and his English partner Davies, to remodel the interior and design a thirty-room attic storey for staff. Mewès was the designer of the London and Paris Ritz hotels and had already been commissioned by Porgès to build a chateau near Paris.

The purchase of Luton Hoo was completed in 1903 and building works commenced in earnest. However, it was now that Julius decided

Newspaper cutting showing an Automobile Club meeting at Luton Hoo, 8 July 1908

he must return to South Africa to review his diamond and gold businesses, leaving Birdie in charge of the extensive building works. Business, as usual, was uppermost in Julius's mind and he could only advise Birdie by letter as best he could:

'Mewès rough estimate was £100,000. I reckoned knowing what rogues they are £150,000 and now you make it £250,000. A fine pickle. Oh the humbug. You must settle as best you can. Have as little done in France as possible.'

All was completed by December 1906 (although the remodelling of the grounds continued) resulting in an Edwardian country house worthy of the wealthiest cosmopolitan society. The architectural historian Nikolaus Pevsner later wrote of Luton Hoo, 'The combination of Edwardian riches with an exacting French training brought about interiors – at Luton Hoo as at the Ritz – which are of the very highest quality in their own terms … At Luton Hoo display was demanded, and it was provided with a panache of which no one after the First World War would have been capable.'

Guests at Luton Hoo included Edward VII, Prince Albert of Schleswig-Holstein, Baron von Strumm, the Marquise d'Hautpane and Grand Duke Michael Michaelovitch of Russia, whose daughter Zia was to marry Julius's second son and heir, Harold, in 1917.

Below: The Wernher's friend Grand Duke Michael of Russia and his daughter Zia, who was to marry Harold Wernher

TOAST LIST.

"The King and Queen."

"The Rest of the Royal Family."

"Our Landlord & the Lord of the Manor."
Proposed by ARTHUR NOTT, Esq.
Responded to by HAROLD WERNHER, Esq.

"The Mayor & Corporation of Luton."
Proposed by H. G. PAPILLON, Esq.
Responded to by HIS WORSHIP THE MAYOR.

"The Luton Hoo Tenants."
Proposed by F. J. MANKIEWICZ, Esq.
Responded to by JOSEPH COLE, Esq.

"Success to Agriculture."
Proposed by H. G. PAPILLON, Esq.
Responded to by HUGH CUMBERLAND, Esq.

"The Chamber of Commerce."
Proposed by GEO. WARREN, Esq.
Responded to by THE PRESIDENT OF THE CHAMBER OF COMMERCE.

"The Foreman of the Jury & the Jury."
Proposed by WILLIAM AUSTIN, Esq.
Responded to by BRUCE PENNY, Esq.

Above: Toast list from the menu for a dinner for tenants, given at Luton Hoo on 24 January 1912

Left: The Long Gallery at Ranger's House showing the Bergonzoli sculpture and the Emperor of China series of tapestries, c.1700

Chinese immigrant workers in the Chinese Compound, Kimberley

Julius, just returned from South Africa, with Alex, 1904

Back to South Africa

As usual, the needs of the business weighed heavily on Julius's mind. Beit had suffered a stroke in Johannesburg in January 1903, and Julius knew that he must prepare to shoulder a greater share of the business. He therefore planned to make a four-month trip to South Africa which would be his first in twenty years. While there, he hoped to be able to determine the scale of investment needed from the backers of his new African Ventures Syndicate. His visit caused great excitement in South Africa – for some it was the first opportunity to meet the famous Julius Wernher in person.

The huge new outputs of the gold mines were to lead to a labour shortage, and by 1903, the time of Julius's visit, labour needs had trebled. He estimated that they would need 30,000 more workers in the next two or three years, but now that the countryside was being cultivated (including fruit farms and vineyards as he diversified investments) the 'kaffirs' preferred to work in the fields. As a 'stopgap'

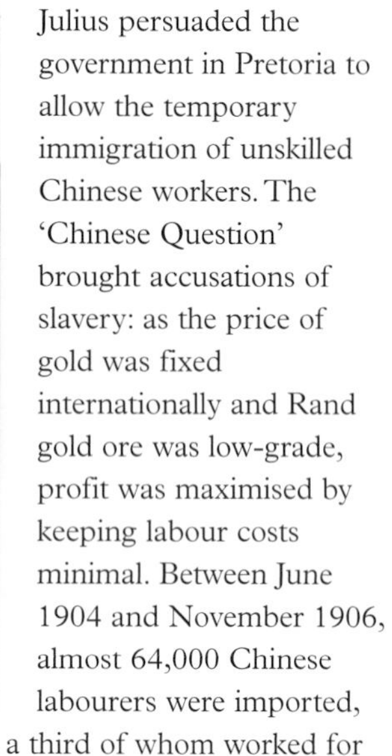

Julius persuaded the government in Pretoria to allow the temporary immigration of unskilled Chinese workers. The 'Chinese Question' brought accusations of slavery: as the price of gold was fixed internationally and Rand gold ore was low-grade, profit was maximised by keeping labour costs minimal. Between June 1904 and November 1906, almost 64,000 Chinese labourers were imported, a third of whom worked for Wernher, Beit and associated companies, under harsh conditions.

The trip came at a bad time as far as Birdie was concerned because it meant that she was left to deal with the huge renovation project at Luton Hoo alone. But for Julius the demands of the business had to come first as usual, and the last decade of his life was to see him so preoccupied with this and the problems and disappointments involving Derrick that he was never able to take any real pleasure in his country house.

Julius was to visit South Africa only once more, on a kind of 'grand tour' in 1909, on which Birdie accompanied him.

Julius on the De Beers travelling car in South Africa, 1909

The Last Years

The death of his greatest friend and business partner, Alfred Beit, aged 53, in 1906, marked a turning-point in Julius's life. The great burden of Julius's business responsibilities, always shared with Beit, were now to be borne alone, and Julius began to suffer from a variety of illnesses and to slide into depression. Sent on a cruise to Egypt to rest in October, he wrote to Birdie, 'My pleasure in business is certainly gone without Beit but the load remains.' On 1 January 1907 he told a friend he would like to 'get out and take the rest of my life easy' but that he continued to persevere because, 'I like to keep up the business for one or two of my boys or sons of partners as I do not approve of the usual style that if a father has made a fortune the sons should become idlers or worse still.' Derrick, now seventeen years old, continued to cause constant trouble at Eton, writing home for money to pay off his large gambling debts.

The Lemoine Affair

It seems ironic that such a discerning businessman as Julius Wernher should have been deceived by two men of no distinction. In both cases his judgement was clouded by personal loyalties. In 1905 Beit had learnt of a French engineer, called Henri Lemoine, who claimed he could mass-produce gem-sized diamonds. Beit visited Lemoine's forge in Paris and returned duly convinced. After Beit's death, Julius decided that, as the sole remaining Life Governor of De Beers, he must buy the rights to Lemoine's formula 'to save the industry'. He secretly agreed to finance the establishment of a factory, hidden in the High Pyrenees, and in 1906, he took the next Chairman of De Beers to meet Lemoine and witness his alchemy. After the demonstration, Julius admitted, 'I am not free of doubt, although we watched like the devil and could not detect foul play.' The payments continued, up to £64,000, but when Julius learnt that a rival had been shown the secret forge in Paris he decided to prosecute Lemoine.

'L'Affaire Lemoine' produced a trial worthy of the theatre. Marcel Proust covered it for *Le Figaro* in a series of humorous literary parodies in the style of Ruskin, Balzac, Flaubert and others. It emerged that Lemoine was indeed a confidence trickster, whose real aim had been to depress the market value of De Beers shares until he could afford to buy some, and then sell them when confidence in the mining industry resumed. Released on bail, Lemoine fled to Sofia, but was arrested and sentenced to six years in gaol. Julius was left exhausted and somewhat humiliated by the ordeal.

Julius Wernher's coat-of-arms aquired when he became a baronet

Left: Julius photographed in Bulawayo, 1909

Newspaper caricature of Wernher relating to the Lemoine Affair

DERRICK

More than anything, it was the behaviour of his favourite son, Derrick, that was to break Julius's heart and bring misery to his last years. Derrick's compulsive gambling, debts and lies were a problem at Eton, but when he moved on to Oxford University, they became worse, and Julius became heavily involved. He wrote of Derrick's behaviour, 'The Lemoine business is nothing to it for this pain will last for ever ...'

To cover debts, Derrick purchased on credit £20,000 worth of jewellery in Bond Street which he took to a pawnbroker in Victoria Street for cash. As usual he sent affectionate, pleading letters home, asking his father 'to make use of your cheque book to some considerable extent in order to put everything right'. A full audit of Derrick's affairs in 1910, when he was twenty-one, revealed debts totalling £35,000 (£1.5 million at today's values). Julius was no longer able to rationalise this behaviour. He wrote to Birdie:

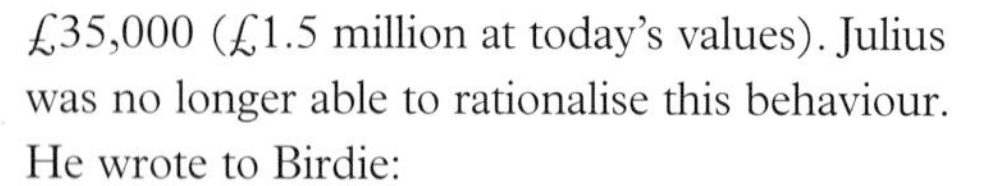

The three brothers (left to right): Alex, Derrick and Harold Wernher

'He is no longer the Eton schoolboy – of course he promises Heaven and Earth to remain straight, but he has no character, never had and I fear never will have. There are things on which I cannot compromise and what is more will not. I am afraid this is a sad letter but I feel hopeless and miserable.'

NOTICE is hereby given, that the Partnership lately subsisting between us, the undersigned, Sir Julius Wernher, Bart., Lionel Phillips, Ludwig Breitmeyer and Friedrich Eckstein, carrying on business at 1, London Wall-buildings, and 29-30, Holborn-viaduct, in the city of London, under the style or firm of WERNHER, BEIT AND CO., has this day been dissolved by mutual consent.—As witness our hands this 31st day of December, 1911.

J. WERNHER.
L. BREITMEYER.
F. ECKSTEIN.
LIONEL PHILLIPS.

036

Notice of the formal liquidation of Wernher, Beit & Co. from the London Gazette, *27 February 1912*

Julius was finally forced to publish notices in the London, Paris and Monte Carlo press disclaiming liability for any of Derrick's bills and finally persuaded him to spend a few months in the Sudan, as assistant to a friend in the Colonial Service. However, on his return Derrick continued as before, and on 12 December 1911 a petition was filed for his bankruptcy; his assets were £225 and his liabilities £81,865.

Birdie's secretary, Margie Pryce, became a very close friend in whom Julius confided at this time, and her letters confirm the seriousness of the effect of Derrick's behaviour on his father. She wrote to Birdie: 'I cannot forgive him for taking so much of the joy of life from his father … whose children were his all in all … How could Derrick destroy all that …'

Heartbroken, in December 1911 Julius announced the voluntary liquidation of Wernher, Beit & Co. The following year he disinherited Derrick in favour of Harold, convinced that his eldest son was 'morally insane'. Derrick made his final appearance in the bankruptcy court in May 1912, and a fortnight later his father died, aged sixty-two, probably from cancer. Julius's body was taken from Bath House to Luton Hoo, and he was buried at the local church at East Hyde. Five thousand people paid their respects along the route. Derrick stayed away, and was arrested in Paris in August for failing to pay debts there. He subsequently moved to New York.

THE LEGACY

As one of the 'Randlords', Julius Wernher had suffered his share of negative publicity during his lifetime. However, his retiring nature and lack of self-advertisement, and the integrity for which he had been respected by those who knew him well, meant that he had not, like Cecil Rhodes and others, become as directly involved in the political scandals of the day. He had remained unaffected by his great wealth and did not value it for itself. Though many were to criticise the mine owners' involvement in South Africa per se, Julius did make sure that he diversified his business interests there in later years to develop housing, transport and farming, and he was proud of these achievements.

"WITHOUT FEAR AND WITHOUT REPROACH."

Vale! Vale!

THE LATE SIR JULIUS WERNHER, BART.

MAY 21st, 1912.

Der Vereinsbote.

Organ des Vereins deutscher Lehrerinnen in England.

No. 3. London, den 15. August 1912. 24. Jahrgang.

Sir Julius Wernher †

Am 21. Mai ist Sir Julius Wernher, der Präsident unseres Vereins und des Herrenkomitees nach langem, schwerem Leiden heimgegangen. Was der Verein in ihm verloren, ist in Worten kaum genugsam auszudrücken. Sir Julius Wernher war alles, was die Welt in seltener Einstimmigkeit von ihm rühmte; aber er war weit mehr, wie alle die wissen, die ihn näher gekannt haben, wie wir in unserem Verein wissen, dem er sein warmes, tätiges Interesse und seine Fürsorge zugewandt hat. Stellte unser Verein auch nur einen sehr kleinen Ausschnitt in dem weiten Umkreise der Interessen von Sir Julius Wernher dar, so gehörte er dennoch in diesen Kreis, und es entsprach der ganzen gewissenhaften Art dieses Mannes, daß es ihm nicht genügte, den Verein durch seinen Namen als Präsident zu ehren, sondern daß er an seiner Hebung und Befestigung praktisch mittätig sein wollte. Vor jetzt 12 Jahren trat er in den Vorstand, dem seine Gemahlin schon angehörte, ein, und wenige Jahre später übernahm er die Präsidentschaft des Herrenkomitees und hat bis zuletzt die Angelegenheiten des Vereins, wo es seine äußere und innere Sicherstellung galt, in sorgfältigster Weise geleitet. Es wird uns, die wir mit ihm zusammenarbeiten durften, unvergeßlich sein, wie er zur Zeit der Erneuerung des Mietskontraktes unserer Häuser die Interessen des Vereins für die Zukunft nach jeder Richtung wahrte und schützte, wie seinen scharfen kritischen Augen nichts entging, woraus dem Verein später möglicherweise ein Nachteil erwachsen konnte. Aber nicht nur auf das Große und Ganze des Vereins erstreckte sich seine Fürsorge. Er wußte, daß oft Fälle der Not und Bedrängnis unter den Mitgliedern vorkommen mußten und gab uns für solche Zwecke jährlich £50, über welche Summe wir nur ihm allein Rechenschaft abzulegen brauchten. Wie viel Gutes damit geschehen, wie viel Tränen auf diese Weise getrocknet wurden, das wissen nur wir, und darin lag die wahre Wohltat, daß Niemand davon erfuhr, und nur wir dem großherzigen Geber danken durften. Wenn Sir Julius gab, so wußte und fühlte man, daß sein großes menschliches Herz mitging. Und das machte den Wert der Gabe für uns aus und gewiß für Alle, denen er half; denn was er in sich selbst war, mußte eben überall durchbrechen. Eine Persönlichkeit von der Bedeutung von Sir Julius, deren Leben sich nur unter großen Bedingungen abspielte und die dennoch Freude und warmes Interesse an einer Arbeit wie die unsrige bis ins Kleinste ...

SIR JULIUS WERNHER.

DEATH OF WELL-KNOWN RAND MAGNATE.

DIAMOND FRAUDS RECALLED.

Sir Julius Wernher, whose name will ever be associated with modern South Africa, died a his London residence last evening. He had been in ill-health for some considerable time past, and the end was not unexpected. The financial caree

Above left: Julius's funeral as illustrated in the South Africa Journal, *1 June 1912*

Above: A goodbye to Julius Wernher in African World, *26 May 1912; obituary of Julius from* Der Vereinsbote, *15 August 1912; and a tribute to Julius published in* The Manchester Courier, *22 May 1912*

His will revealed the variety and scale of his interests as a philanthropist. Provisionally estimated at £11.5 million his estate was then the largest ever recorded by the Inland Revenue. After many bequests, death duties were estimated at £850,000. His painting by Watteau, *La Gamme d'Amour*, was left to the National Gallery, but there were no grand schemes for a museum for his art collection; it was simply left in trust to his son Harold. Birdie was left Bath House and its contents for life, together with the contents of Luton Hoo. Had his last years not been so troubled, Julius might have had time to plan for its future. Like the Beit Collection (now at Russborough, near Dublin, and in the National Gallery of Ireland), the Wernher Collection became a family responsibility.

Apart from his art collection, the most prominent legacy of Julius Wernher in London today is the Imperial College of Science and Technology. Huge busts of Julius and Alfred Beit, each supported by allegorical figures, flank its main entrance in Prince Consort Road, South Kensington. They were also the largest benefactors of The King Edward VII Hospital, now in Beaumont Street, in west London. Demonstrating the generosity of a successful immigrant he made legacies to the German Hospital in London, the German Benevolent Society and the Society for Foreigners in Distress. The hospital and children's home in Luton were among several local beneficiaries. In South Africa Wernher left funds to build and endow a university, and donations to the Kimberley Hospital and the German School at Johannesburg. He had previously donated funds and four paintings (by Géricault, Falguiere and two by Millais) to help the founders of the National Gallery of South Africa in Johannesburg. His most unusual legacy, however, is the collection of works of art that several generations of his family have shared with the public.

Busts sculpted by P R Montford of Julius Wernher and Alfred Beit still flank the entrance to the Imperial College of Science and Technology in Kensington, founded in 1907 with a donation from Wernher, Beit & Co.

JEWELLERY

Enamelled gold pendant with a youth standing among seven large flower heads set with rose diamonds and enamelled in colours. Late 17th century, probably northern European

The jewellery collected by Julius Wernher comprises approximately 115 enamelled, jewelled, and chased gold pieces, dating from the second century BC up to the nineteenth century. About two thirds of the pieces in the collection dates from the Renaissance period (sixteenth and seventeenth centuries). The remainder were either made in the eighteenth century, or in the nineteenth in a Renaissance style (such as the lizard pendant, which was probably made in the 1820s). The earliest item is the Greek earring of the winged figure of Victory, made from the purest and softest gold.

A feature of the jewellery collection is the marvellous enamelwork it includes – a tribute to the goldsmiths and craftsmen who made these objects. Jewellers of the Renaissance period would be obliged to join the craftsmen's guild to which goldsmiths were required to belong – the Guild of Saint Dunstan. In order to gain entry to the guild, each jeweller would submit their examination piece – the 'masterpiece'.

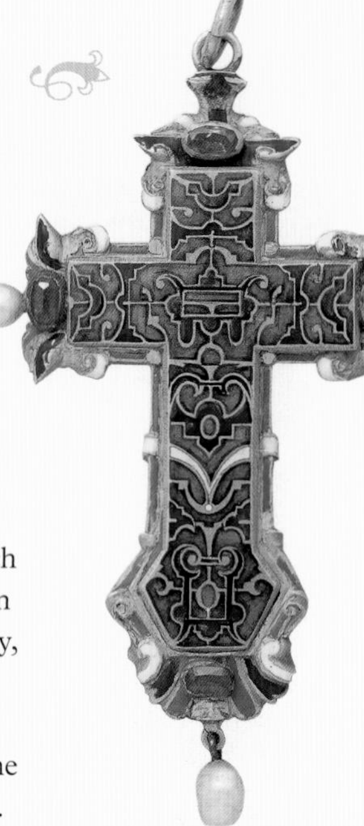

Silver-gilt double-armed cross, with 22 garnets and 3 hanging pearls and enamelled with the instruments of the Crucifixion, 19th century

Right: Gold ring with three ruby hearts and the words, 'Ye three'. Inscribed around the hoop the words, 'Gay, Discreet, Secret', possibly telling the story of a lady choosing between three suitors, 18th century

Left and below: Gourd-shaped pomander of four sections set with twelve rubies on an enamelled coloured ground of fruit and flowers with a hanging pearl. Dutch or German, c.1630

Right: Baroque pearl forming the body of a cherub, with enamel wings and back. The large pearl is suspended by two chains. Made in Germany in the 17th century

A manuscript survives from 1579, entitled the *'Libris de Passanties'*, which shows drawings of the apprentices' entry pieces. The kind of pieces represented are very similar to many of those in Julius Wernher's collection.

The main categories of jewellery represented in the collection are cameos, reliquary pendants, rings, religious jewels, memorial jewels (portrait pendants and rings) and *memento mori* jewels. *Memento mori* pieces, such as the skull pendant, were meant as a reminder of the transience of life. There are also pieces of jewellery meant purely for decoration, often designed to be worn by men as well as women.

We know from an inventory of 1913 that the jewels were not displayed by Julius, but stored in a vault in leather drawers. However, like the other areas of Julius's collection, the individual pieces were chosen for their particularly fine craftsmanship.

The very best ring in the collection, and outstanding in its own right, this ring is set with large diamonds, and rectangular cut diamonds all round the hoop exterior. The inside is painstakingly enamelled with black enamel scrollwork, late 16th century

Gold pendant of an opal-set lizard with ruby collar and eyes, 19th century

Below: Miniature skull pendant on an enamelled foliate device hung with two pendant pearls, 17th century

Above: Enamelled gold pendant hinging open to reveal a miniature scene of the baptism of Christ, 17th century

Right: Greek earring of the winged figure of Victory, made of gold. The earliest piece of jewellery in the collection, dating from the 2nd century BC

Right: Gold circular pendant set with rectangular cut diamonds and openwork leaves (right). The reverse (left) is exquisitely decorated with blue, green and white 'peapod' enamelling, Spanish, c.1630

MEDIEVAL

Virgin and Child *by Hans Memling (1430/40–94)*

The intricate craftsmanship and quality of execution that had always inspired Julius Wernher in his work and his collecting were presumably the attributes that drew him to the great craftsmanship of the Medieval period. Much of his collection consists of ivories, woodcarvings, religious metalwork, pictures and tapestries from this period.

Most medieval works were made for the Church, the greatest patron of the arts in medieval times. They were created by respected craftsmen, usually monks, for whom they were a labour of love and an act of worship. Julius commented that some of these pieces had been handled 'by stronger and more thoughtful workers' than the artists represented in the collections of more conventional connoisseurs. Julius's German birth and Lutheran upbringing may also account for the fact that many of the works he chose to collect are religious and of northern European origin. The northern European works placed less emphasis on

Late 15th-century French or Flemish ivory plaque depicting Christ as the Man of Sorrows, rising from the tomb flanked by angels

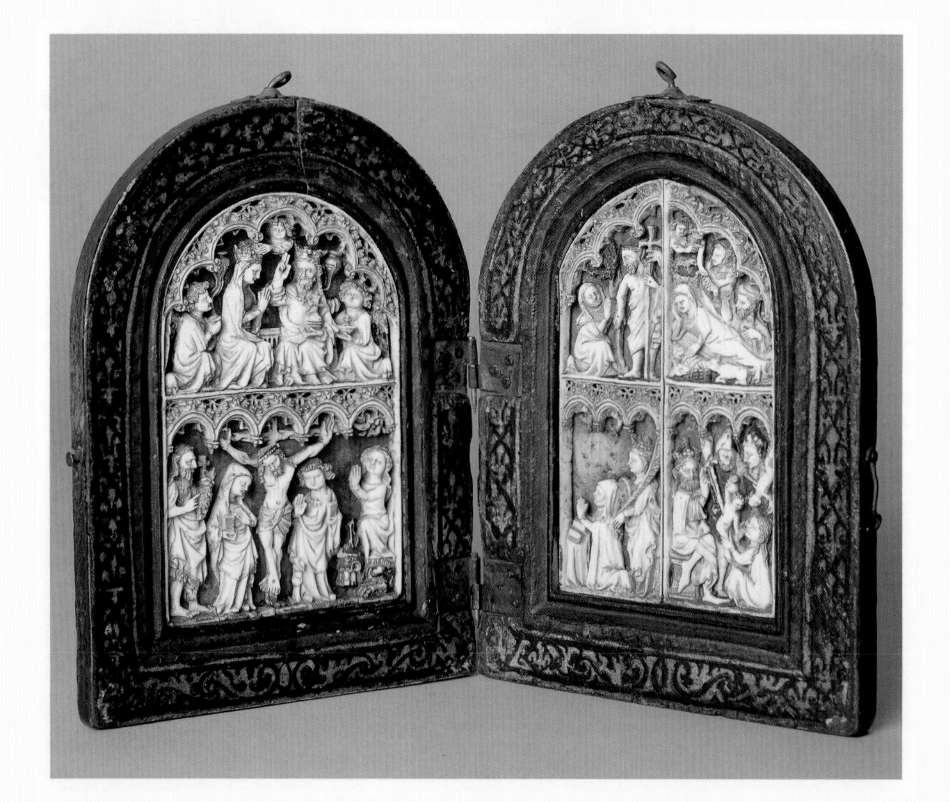

Left: French diptych formed from delicately coloured and gilded ivory panels depicting scenes from the life of Christ, set into a painted wooden case, itself painted with the baptism of Christ and the Annunciation. Designed as an altarpiece for private devotional use, 14th century

Below: A carved circular draughts-piece made from red-stained walrus tusk showing Samson destroying the temple of the Philistines, 12th century

perspective, in favour of graphic, rather stark depictions of figures and landscapes that portray their message with great emotional impact.

After the jewellery collection, ivories may have been Julius's main enthusiasm. Precious materials were more usually used by craftsmen, and in the Middle Ages ivory was as valuable as gold or gemstones, with the added attraction that it came from an exotic beast that most people had never seen. Fifty-five examples displayed at Ranger's House range from the seventh to the fourteenth centuries and include caskets, book covers, ceremonial church objects and domestic shrines in the form of small folding altarpieces of two, three or more leaves (diptychs, triptychs and polyptychs). As well as Virgin and Child subjects, Crucifixions, and elegant Annunciation scenes carved in low relief, there is a group of secular scenes, mainly carved in Paris from the fourteenth century on jewel caskets, mirror cases and writing tablets.

Above: Large 16th-century Flemish memento mori *pommel, once part of a sword hilt. Carved on one side with a young woman and on the other with a worm-eaten corpse inscribed 'Ecce Finem'*

Right: Single illuminated leaf from a missal showing the Madonna and Child with saints and kneeling worshippers. The bottom panel has been taken from another book and attached to the picture above with a linen strip. The blue colour is crushed lapis lazuli, which was reserved for the portrayal of the most sacred figures, Perugia, 1320s

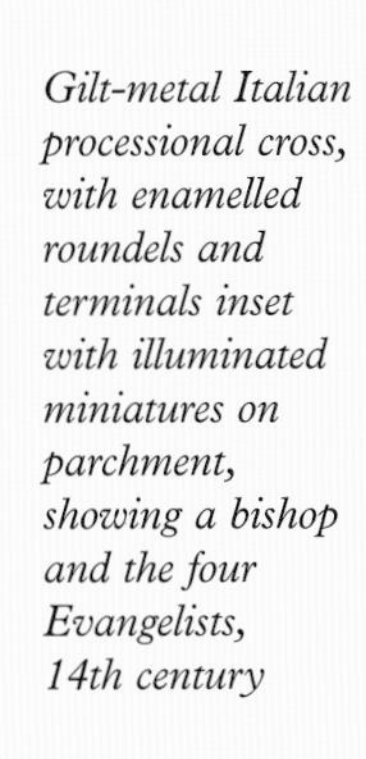

Gilt-metal Italian processional cross, with enamelled roundels and terminals inset with illuminated miniatures on parchment, showing a bishop and the four Evangelists, 14th century

Right: Limoges enamel book cover, in lustrous shades of blue, turquoise and green, with a blue and white border, mounted with a copper-gilt figure of Christ seated in majesty, 13th century

Tapestry panel made in the Southern Netherlands, c.*1500, depicting the head of Christ on a spandrelled silver-thread ground*

Above: French circular ivory mirror case carved in relief showing a knight and his lady playing chess at a table in a tent. Some traces of the original red, blue and green colouring can still be seen. Early 14th century

Right: Gilt-metal and enamel reliquary. A large oblong casket with four champlevé *enamel figures, circular bosses and oval, round and rectangular stones. The back is inset with a later gilt-metal plaque with birds and scrolling foliage, on four winged animal feet. This reliquary demonstrates the popularity of Gothic arts in the Victorian period – 13th-century enamelled panels have been applied to a 19th-century box decorated in the style of a medieval reliquary*

RENAISSANCE

Below: A Limoges circular plaque depicting the Judgement of Paris, painted en grisaille *with a tiny representation of the abduction of Helen and a border decorated with figures, arabesques and scrolling foliage, by Martial Ydeux dit le Pape, mid-1540s*

Julius found the rich variety of Renaissance art as attractive as that of the medieval period. The Renaissancce examples differ from the medieval pieces in their subject matter. From the mid-sixteenth century, artists began to be funded more by secular patrons, and their work reflected secular, as well as religious, subjects. As a lover of fine craftsmanship, Wernher seems to have appreciated the technical advances that influenced craftsmen of sixteenth- and seventeenth-century Europe, particularly in metalwork and ceramics. He formed one of the finest private collections of Renaissance bronzes, and the seventy-five examples on display illustrate the virtuosity the medium demands, from casting to finishing with chasing and patination. Forms include statuettes, busts, medallions, plaquettes, candlesticks, inkstands, lamps, bells and doorknobs.

No less rich in variety are the ceramics, with four examples of the bizarre dishes produced by the French potter Bernard Palissy and twenty-six examples of maiolica

Maiolica dish in vibrant colours, from around 1530, with a portrait of Portia

Below: Madonna and Child with Saints *by a follower of Francesco Francia (c.1450–1517/18)*

Right: Wood and enamel altarpiece, made around 1600, supported with two twisted rock crystal columns and set with a large verre eglomisé *plaque of Mary, Joseph and Saint John with the Christ child, surrounded by 19 further plaques depicting the life of Christ*

Pair of bronze plaquettes showing scenes from the life of Christ by Francesco Fanelli (active 1608–1661), Florence, mid-17th century. The upper plaque depicts the encounter with the robber during the Flight into Egypt and the lower one shows Christ on the road to Calvary

(tin-glazed earthenware). These range from apothecaries' drug jars to two rare plates from the celebrated dinner service made by Nicola da Urbino for the great Mantuan collector Isabella d'Este, around 1525. The colours of these, and of the jewel-like Limoges enamels, provide a sparkling display. The intense colours of Limoges were produced by painting on copper, and the collection contains some fascinating examples in the form of decorative plaques and roundels, as well as salt cellars, mirror cases, dishes and even a spoon.

Most of the Renaissance metalwork in the collection is either German or Flemish and was probably collected by Wernher when he visited his family in Germany. An intriguing theme in the collection is the recurrence of animals and birds, for example in the form of drinking cups with removable heads. The most endearing is undoubtedly a coconut cup mounted with silver-gilt as a crowned owl by a Nuremberg silversmith in the nineteenth century, following an early seventeenth-century design.

Limoges rectangular plaque, set into a gilt-metal frame, showing a bearded man with long yellow hair, identified as a Reformer. Possibly from the workshop of Limousin, c.1550

Left: Coconut cup mounted with silver-gilt as a crowned owl, 19th-century German replica of an early 17th-century design

Below: Italian bronze figure of Hercules lying pillowed on a wineskin, Bologna, c.1500. An inscription on the underside records this as having been made for Gaspare Fantuzzi, a Bolognese nobleman

Left: A pair of armorial dishes from the Gonzaga Este service, painted by Nicola da Urbino. From a famous service of 22 plates made c.*1528 for Isabella d'Este, wife of Gianfrancesco Gonzaga, Marchese di Mantova*

Right: The Holy Family *by Gian-Francesco Maineri (active 1489–1504) including, in the background, statues of Adam and Eve. One of only a handful of works known to be by this artist*

Left: Gilt-metal ostrich with pearl pendant collar and exquisitely detailed base with a tiny pig and other wildlife in reeds, 17th century

Bronze bust of Minerva with silvered eyes, possibly by Aurelio Lombardo, (c.*1501–63)*

Ranger's House

EARLY RESIDENTS

FRANCIS HOSIER (1700–1727)

(Dates given refer to the residents' period of occupancy)

Captain Francis Hosier (1673–1727) built the brick villa now known as Ranger's House around 1700. Born nearby in Deptford, then a naval shipbuilding town, he rose to become Vice-Admiral of the Blue. However, he probably owed his fortune to investing in ships' cargoes or to booty gained from capturing other ships. The carved stone mask of Neptune over the front door alludes to the ship of the same name on which he served as a nineteen-year-old lieutenant in 1692 and to another ship from which much of his income derived.

Hosier chose to live in an area popular with seafaring men, both for ready access to the sea via the Thames and on account of the Royal Naval Hospital, built by Christopher Wren from 1694. In 1724 Daniel Defoe observed that Greenwich was favoured by 'gentlemen still in Service, as in the Navy Ordnance Docks, Yards &c, as well while in Business, as after laying down their Employment'. The house was the first to be built near the Royal Observatory (constructed in 1695) on the Greenwich Meridian Line. One may picture the admiral climbing the spiral wooden stairs (still in existence, though not open to visitors) up to the flat, balustraded roof of his villa, to enjoy peering through his telescope down to Greenwich to watch the ships come in, or admire the fine prospects across the royal park. He purchased from the widow of the first Astronomer Royal, John Flamsteed, his book of observations of star positions, *Historiae Coelestis* (1712, rev. ed. 1725) which suggests that he may also have enjoyed studying the stars at night from his lead roof.

Hosier employed at least eight servants, who worked and slept in the basement. However, he never retired to Greenwich, for in 1725 he was sent to the West Indies to blockade Spanish treasure ships and, following an outbreak of yellow fever, he was among 4000 men who died at Porto Bello in 1727. In 1739 Admiral Vernon's capture of the same Panama port inspired the popular ballad 'Admiral Hosier's Ghost'. Hosier's body was interred in the family vault at St Nicholas, Deptford.

An inventory of the contents of the house, drawn up in 1728, records damask hangings, silvered furniture, oriental rugs, family portraits, engravings and exotic curiosities from his travels such as bows and arrows, and a straw hammock. Hosier had married in 1710 and had a daughter, but his mother's relations began a lengthy lawsuit to gain possession, and some ten years after his death they finally succeeded. By 1740 they sold a lease to John Stanhope (1704–48), the younger brother of Philip, fourth Earl of Chesterfield, who became a Commissioner of the Admiralty in 1748, shortly before his death.

CHESTERFIELD HOUSE (1748–73)

Lord Chesterfield (1694–1773) is the most celebrated resident of Ranger's House. Inheriting the villa in 1748 from his younger brother, he would have sold the seven-year lease that remained, but realised 'I could not part with it, but to a very great loss, considering the sums of money that he had laid out upon it.' He would have preferred a villa upstream near Richmond or Twickenham, near his good friend Mrs Howard at Marble Hill. That same year

Opposite: Ranger's House, painted in 1884 by Anthony de Bree (active 1882–1913), Museum of London. Showing the covered portico added for the first resident Ranger, Princess Sophia Matilda

Left: The carved stone mask of Neptune over the front door of Ranger's House

Above: Philip, fourth Earl of Chesterfield, aged 76, after Thomas Gainsborough. The Earl was the most famous resident of Ranger's House

Chesterfield resigned from the government in protest at foreign policy. He had served as Ambassador to The Hague from 1728–32 and in 1745, as Lord Lieutenant of Ireland 1745–6, and then as Secretary of State for the Northern Department (the name then given to Scotland and the north of England) from 1746–8. His sights were now set on creating a magnificent Mayfair residence, Chesterfield House, built by Isaac Ware in South Audley Street in 1749 (demolished in 1934).

He soon grew to love his inherited villa. An avid collector of great paintings, works of art and furniture, Chesterfield initially 'destined' the villa 'for the pleasures of society'. He remodelled the central dining room and added a long gallery, vowing 'my great room will be full of pictures as it ought to be; and all capital ones'. It was probably also built by Ware. Seventy-seven feet long and twenty-two wide, it almost doubled the area of Hosier's house and encroached, illegally, through the park wall. When he applied for a full fifty-year renewal of his crown lease in 1766, the encroachment was discovered and the annual fee was set at £10, compared to six shillings and eight pence for the rest of the house and gardens.

As a society house, Chesterfield's villa was short-lived, for in 1752 he went deaf. However, in April 1753 he wrote, 'I am now, for the first time in my life, impatient for summer, that I may go and hide myself at Blackheath and converse with my vegetables.' Withdrawing from aristocratic and intellectual society, Chesterfield devoted himself not only to his vegetables at Blackheath but also to his correspondence with friends such as Voltaire. One of the greatest letter-writers of all time, Chesterfield is best known for his letters to his illegitimate son and, after his death in 1768, to his godson and heir, both of whom were named Philip Stanhope. Written to guide these young men towards worldly advancement as diplomats, courtiers or politicians, one set of letters was published the year after Chesterfield's death by his illegitimate son's secret widow. It became an instant international bestseller (and, judging from sales figures, Chesterfield's *Letters* are best known today not in English but in Japanese translation).

Below: Portrait of Philip Stanhope *by John Russell. Philip or 'Sturdy' (to become the fifth Earl of Chesterfield) was the recipient of the famous letters from the fourth Earl*

Chesterfield married but had no children, and after his death his godson inherited the house and title. The fifth Earl (1755–1815) lived here only occasionally and in 1782, the year before he sold the house, Christie's auctioned the contents. Their catalogue reveals the collections of the fourth Earl, with suites of carved and gilt French Rococo furniture, French clocks, busts, marble-topped side tables, silk festoon curtains and a connoisseur's collection of paintings.

'Sturdy', as the fourth Earl called his godson and heir, had been an endearing child; he is recorded at the house in 1763, when he was eight, learning Latin with Chesterfield and beating his valet, Walsh, at draughts. But his tutor was hanged for forging his signature and by the time of his inheritance he was heavily in debt. In 1781, when the Prince of Wales came to dinner at the house, the guard dog Towzer attacked a footman and the Prince and the Earl fell down the front steps, the Prince injuring his head.

RICHARD HULSE
(1783–1805)

Another collector, Richard Hulse (1727–1805) purchased the house and gradually filled it with paintings, to judge from the catalogue of a two-day sale held by Christie's in 1806. A barrister and Deputy Governor of the Hudson Bay Company of Canada, he built the north wing of the house to balance the gallery on the entrance front. After his death the remainder of his lease was purchased by John Symmonds, who assigned it in 1807 to the sister of King George III, Augusta, Dowager Duchess of Brunswick.

PRIVATE COLLECTION

Right: Richard Hulse, by Francis Cotes (1726–70), 1761

A 'Grace and Favour' Residence

The Duchess of Brunswick (1807–13)

In 1806 George III appointed Caroline, Princess of Wales, to the sinecure position of Ranger of Greenwich Park. The princess was the daughter of Princess Augusta, and thus the King's niece as well as his daughter-in-law. Formally estranged from the Prince of Wales since 1796, she had been living since 1799 at Montagu House, next door to the present Ranger's House. With mother and daughter now adjacent, their gardens were connected, and 15 acres of the royal park were enclosed to afford privacy. In 1808 engravings of both houses appeared in *The Lady's Magazine*, which described the gardens as the work of John Meader, who later created an 'English Garden' in Russia for Catherine the Great. The villa's name now changed from Chesterfield House to Brunswick House. Continuing the tradition of this collectors' house, Princess Augusta brought fine paintings which were the subject of an auction on the premises (the third in thirty years) held by Phillips after her death in 1813.

The following year, the Princess of Wales left England. Montagu House was demolished (the site is now covered by tennis courts) and the land incorporated into the grounds of the present villa, which was purchased by the Crown to serve as the new official residence of the Ranger.

Princess Sophia Matilda (1815–44)

In 1815 Princess Sophia Matilda (1773–1844), an unmarried niece of George III, became the first Ranger to live at Ranger's House. The gallery was divided into three rooms, and a covered portico was added to link the front door to Chesterfield Walk. Along with extensive repairs and redecoration, new water closets were installed. A collector's cabinet, made by George Bullock, was purchased for the house in 1995. Presented to Princess Sophia by Queen Charlotte in August 1814 it may have been intended to commemorate her appointment. Princess Sophia lived here for longer than anyone, and in 1844 her elaborate funeral prompted several engravings in the illustrated press. Once again, the contents of the house are recorded in a catalogue of an auction, in which the cabinet appears, held on the premises over three days in 1845.

George, fourth Earl of Aberdeen (1784–1860), was the second Ranger to be granted the house, in 1845. Prime Minister from 1852 to 1854, he handed the house over to his son, Lord Haddo, and his family, who left in 1855. Lord Canning, on his retirement as Governor General of India, was offered the post of Ranger and the house by Queen Victoria in 1861 but within months he and his wife had died.

Prince Arthur of Connaught (1862–73)

In 1862 Queen Victoria's third son, Prince Arthur, came to live here, aged twelve, with his tutor, to study for a place at the Royal Military Academy, Woolwich, which he secured in 1866. Prince Arthur constructed miniature forts in the

The Duchess of Brunswick in an engraving by Maria Anne Bourlier for La Belle Assemblée, *1 January 1808*

THE ROYAL ARCHIVES© QUEEN ELIZABETH II

Prince Arthur of Connaught with companions, c.1868. The Prince is seated on the right, flanked by the standing figures of his tutor at Ranger's House, Lt. Col. Elphingstone (left), and his equerry, Lieutenant Pickard (right)

MARY EVANS PICTURE LIBRARY

An engraving showing the elaborate funeral of Princess Sophia in 1844 with Ranger's House in the background

Field-Marshal Lord Wolseley, Commander-in-Chief of the Army

Ranger's House in 1937, when it was leased as a tea room

grounds (probably similar to the ones at his childhood home, Osborne House, Isle of Wight). He had the use of the house until he was aged twenty-two, during his years at Woolwich and on military service in Canada.

From 1877–88 the position of Ranger was filled by Blanche, Countess of Mayo, widow of the Viceroy of India who had been assassinated in 1872.

Field-Marshal Lord Wolseley (1888–96)

In 1888 General Lord Wolseley accepted the position offered by Queen Victoria, and occupied the house, commissioning alterations from the fashionable church architect G F Bodley. Lord Wolseley also filled the house with an art collection, but one that included 'military and sporting trophies' from his service around the world. Retired from active service (which had included the expedition to relieve General Gordon at Khartoum), he worked at the War Office before moving to Dublin in 1890 as Commander-in-Chief.

After eighty years of varied use as a grace and favour residence, the house saw no new Rangers cross its threshold. In 1897 Queen Victoria presented it to the Commissioners of Woods and Forests in exchange for the restoration of Kensington Palace.

Ranger's House in the Twentieth Century

The lease was then sold, in 1902, to the London County Council (the same year as the LCC acquired Marble Hill in Twickenham as a public park). The house opened to the public as tea rooms serving Greenwich Park and Blackheath, with toilets and changing facilities for the tennis courts. Requisitioned during the Second World War, the house was restored architecturally between 1959 and 1960 and was then used for local history exhibitions, organised by the Blackheath Society, with the LCC architects' offices upstairs. In 1974 Ranger's House reopened as a gallery for the Suffolk Collection of English portraits and old master paintings, formerly part of the family collection of the Earls of Suffolk and Berkshire. The house and collection passed from the Greater London Council to English Heritage in 1986.

Ranger's House is of no particular architectural distinction, but it is a good example of its kind with most of its original panelled interiors and later extensions intact. Although the house had been home to many collections of note, none of them survived complete, or could be reassembled. For this reason, in the 1990s, when English Heritage had the opportunity to save the Wernher Collection from dispersal, it seemed fitting to install it at Ranger's House, giving the Collection a new home, and the house another new lease of life.

One of the reception rooms in Ranger's House today, decorated to suggest the Pink Drawing Room at Bath House where the Wernher Collection originally lived